Background

The President's Advisory Council on Financial Capability (PACFC) was created by Executive Order 13530, signed by President Barack Obama on January 29, 2010. Its charter is to advise the President on promoting and enhancing financial literacy and capability among the American people.

While the PACFC cannot by federal statute become operational, it is charged with providing financial capability policy recommendations for the nation to the President of the United States. The Partnerships Subcommittee and the Subcommittee on the Underserved and Community Empowerment encourage public- and private-sector collaboration to strengthen the financial capability of Americans in communities throughout the country.

One priority of the PACFC is to encourage the creation of state, tribal and local financial capability initiatives to build financial security for individuals and economic well-being for their communities at large.

What is *financial capability*?

Executive Order 13530, which established the PACFC, defines financial capability as the capacity, based on knowledge, skills and access, to manage financial resources effectively.

The purpose of this document

The goal of this document is to inspire local leaders to leverage partnerships to create their own financial capability initiatives as a means toward building financial well-being in their communities – a prerequisite for competing and winning in a global economy.

This document serves as a resource guide and a roadmap to help regional, state, tribal and local leaders get started with their own financial capability initiatives. While it provides many specific examples of impactful work happening around the country, this document is intended for reference only, and is not intended to endorse or promote specific initiatives.

Why State, Tribal and Local Leadership Matters

Local leaders in states, tribes, local governments and communities play a critical role in helping people improve their financial capability. Because local leaders have a unique understanding of the economic, financial and educational obstacles that negatively impact the people in their communities, they are in a strong position to drive local strategies and initiatives that can make a real difference.

Many states, tribes and local governments are already leading the charge and have made significant and measurable impact. Some examples include, but are certainly not limited to, the states of Delaware and Wisconsin; the cities of San Francisco, Miami, New York, and Savannah, Georgia; and American Indian Tribes such as Citizen Potawatomi Nation in Oklahoma and Eastern Band of Cherokee Indians in North Carolina, among others.

Successful states, tribes and localities leverage existing resources and infrastructure – and they utilize partnerships across the public, private and nonprofit sectors – to implement innovative programs that improve the financial well-being and outcomes of their citizens. They have clear objectives, well-defined program implementation and marketing strategies, and outcomes-driven metrics. Successful jurisdictions also share their findings, best-practices, and challenges with other communities.

The PACFC has identified three broad areas for financial capability initiatives:

- Financial education and capability programs for youth,

- Financial capability and access for low- to moderate-income families and the underserved,

- Financial capability in the workplace.

This document is organized to help communities address these critical areas.

Key steps to creating local fnancial capability initiatives

Step 1:
Evaluate the local landscape, and make a case for addressing financial capability

To build local support and develop working partnerships to advance financial capability in communities, stakeholders need to understand why financial capability is an important issue, what's currently being done in the community to address the issue, what's at stake in communities with poor financial health, and how strong financial behaviors and outcomes among community members can have a positive impact on a community's overall economic health.

It's important to begin by evaluating the current landscape. Conduct an inventory of organizations and programs that are already involved with or are addressing financial empowerment initiatives, such as financial literacy and education, asset-building, financial coaching, tax-preparation assistance, and anything else related to financial capability. Keep in mind that many banks and foundations fund this type of work at the local level, so it may make sense to find out which initiatives have been successful, and include representatives from those initiatives in the discussion.

Key elements of a business case could include:

a. Your state's performance on the FINRA Investor Education Foundation's National Financial Capability Study, where you'll find how your state compares to other states and the nation as a whole on five measures: spending vs. saving, emergency savings, non-bank borrowing, financial literacy, and comparison shopping: usfinancialcapability.org

b. Your state's performance on the CFED (Corporation for Enterprise Development) Assets & Opportunity Scorecard, a state-by-state performance and policy analysis on five areas: Financial Assets & Income, Businesses & Jobs, Housing & Homeownership, Health Care and Education: cfed.org/scorecard

c. Local rates of "unbanked"/"underbanked" individuals
Research your community at webtools.joinbankon.org/community/search

d. Local foreclosure rates. Websites such as realtytrac.com can provide statistics.

e. Local performance on financial capability among the general population and/
or specific segments such as youth and workers. Local/state insights may be
culled from national studies and resources, including:

    i. Employee Benefit Research Institute: ebri.org

    ii. Gallup Hope Index: www.operationhope.org/page/pgid/39

    iii. Jump$tart Coalition for Personal Financial Literacy: jumpstart.org

    iv. State-by-state results on the National Financial Capability Challenge:
    challenge.treas.gov

f. Information and testimonials about how other communities have embraced
financial capability and improved the financial well-being of their citizens. Some
examples include Delaware, Wisconsin, New York City, San Francisco, Indianapolis,
San Antonio, Seattle-King County, Savannah, Providence, American Indian and
Alaska Native Tribes, and many others. (See Resource Guide/Appendix.)

Step 2:
Create a Local Council

A local financial literacy/financial capability council is a formalized group of influential individuals representing governments, education leaders, nonprofit organizations, academia, private foundations, and private industry who agree to serve voluntarily with the collective goal of enhancing financial literacy and capability among the state, tribe or local community.

Potential benefits of creating a local council:

- **Builds efficiency** by sharing information and resources across multiple organizations with similar goals.

- **Encourages innovation** by bringing unique points of view and areas of expertise to the table.

- **Helps communities set strategic priorities** through collaboration and cross-institutional partnership.

- **Maximizes resources by pooling human and financial capital** to jointly solve problems and minimize duplicative programs in local areas.

- **Creates greater visibility and cross-community support** by helping to ensure that resources are focused where the impact can be greatest.

Who should lead and be part of a council?

Councils can take many shapes and sizes. In fact, it's critical that they be customized to the unique needs and circumstances of the local community. Members of the PACFC held meetings and learning sessions with state and city councils and leaders to identify common practices that lead to successful local efforts. Through those discussions, several common themes and recommendations emerged.

By and large, experts agree that councils can be most effective when they include influential leaders and decision-makers, such as the following:

- Government leaders, both elected and high-level career staff, who can prioritize public resources and leverage a "bully pulpit" to improve visibility and awareness of the issues and solutions.

- Education leaders, including school superintendents, who can effect change within the existing education infrastructure and among local youth.

- Financial education experts, including nonprofit and community-based organizations, professional associations, Cooperative Extension services and others with expertise in delivering financial education and capability content. Examples include the Financial Planning Association (FPA), the National Association of Personal Financial Advisors (NAPFA) and the Association for Financial Counseling, Planning and Education (AFCPE).

- Nonprofit organizations, libraries, and other community service providers with expertise serving specific populations such as youth, underserved individuals and low- to moderate-income families.

- Academics and researchers, who bring extensive knowledge, data, and objective analysis of what works and what does not.

- Local business leaders, particularly those from financial institutions such as banks and credit unions, who bring business and financial acumen, product-development expertise, and financial and professional (pro bono) resources.

- Local community members who may be struggling with financial instability themselves, or who may offer practical insights on the issues and concerns of community members.

- Other stakeholders who can share unique perspectives, such as youth leaders, retirees, and other engaged residents.

For a step-by-step guide to getting a Financial Literacy Council off the ground in your community, see "**Steps for Launching a Local Financial Literacy/Financial Capability Council**," in the appendix.

Step 3:
Focus the work

Determine key areas of focus for the jurisdiction's financial capability work and then establish committees or working teams to be responsible for each area of focus. Each jurisdiction will have unique priorities. However, the PACFC recommends three broad areas that will be relevant to any community:

1. Youth financial education and capability,

2. Financial access for the underserved,

3. Financial capability through the workplace.

Step 4:
Articulate clear goals and metrics

Create a core list of financial literacy and financial capability goals and objectives that will drive positive outcomes and enhance the lives of community members.

Following is a sample, noncomprehensive list of example goals and metrics:

- *Every public high-school student in [jurisdiction] will participate in the National Financial Capability Challenge beginning in 20XX.*

- *Every public school student in [jurisdiction] will complete financial capability education upon graduation, beginning with the class of 20XX.*

- *50% of all employers in [jurisdiction] will voluntarily implement financial education that aligns with U.S. Treasury Department's Core Competencies by 20XX.*

- *[Jurisdiction] will reduce the rate of unbanked individuals by 60% over 5 years.*

- *[Jurisdiction] will reduce the foreclosure rate by 40% within the next 18 months.*

Step 5:
Develop and launch programs
that address the stated goals

Consider adopting some of the following programs and initiatives, many of which have been successfully implemented in other jurisdictions. The initiatives are organized under the PACFC's three core areas of focus: financial education for youth, financial capability and access for the underserved, and financial capability in the workplace.

Financial education for youth

1. Encourage and/or incentivize your school district to develop a K-12 plan to fully integrate curriculum that is aligned with what young people need to know, at what ages, in order to become financially capable. Developing strategies to align this work with goals established by the Common Core – and integrating appropriate teacher training – should be included. At the same time, encourage outside learning with organizations like Junior Achievement, Boys & Girls Clubs of America, Lemonade Day, and Savings Plans with Incentives.

   Resources to support these plans, as well as information concerning state mandates and local resources, can be found at jumpstart.org and councilforeconed.org. "Money Milestones'" is another useful resource and can be accessed at moneyasyougrow.org.

2. Establish programs in public schools to ensure all students have the knowledge necessary to undertake financial planning for college and career goals, including:

   · Financial management for working youth,

   · Ensuring students understand the connection between education and potential income,

   · Ensuring college-bound students understand the FAFSA form, reduce their exposure to higher interest private loans, and maximize their capture of federal loans.

The U.S. Department of Education FAFSA website provides resources at fafsa.ed.gov/. John Hancock High School in Chicago is an example of the impact of such programs. Counselors at the school helped students access about $3.5 million in grants and financial aid last year, up from $5,000 just a few years earlier. The school's college enrollment rate has also increased from 49 percent in 2008 to 80 percent in 2010.

3. Encourage and/or incentivize local high schools to participate in the National Financial Capability Challenge, which raises awareness about the need for financial capability efforts and is sponsored by the U.S. Department of Treasury and recommended by the PACFC. Participating students and schools are eligible for scholarships and grants.

   · Learn more about the National Financial Capability Challenge at challenge.treas.gov

4. Ensure that youth summer jobs provided by the state, tribe or local government incorporate direct deposit, savings accounts, and financial capability and financial literacy training.

   · The Economics Awareness Council in Chicago implemented such an initiative. Learn more at econcouncil.org.

5. Encourage local youth-services organizations to adopt programs that deliver financial education. Examples include:

   · Boys & Girls Clubs of America's Money Matters: Make It Count: moneymattersmakeitcount.com

   · Junior Achievement: ja.org

   · Boys Scouts and Girls Scouts personal finance badges: scouting.org, girlscouts.org

Financial capability access for the underserved

1. Conduct an assessment of your community's needs and identify local barriers to financial stability for residents. Consider evaluating the number of unbanked individuals, as well as whether and why individuals are using "alternative" banking services such as pay-day lenders and check-cashing services. This information will help inform the types of programs, products and services that may be needed in your community.

2. Set targets for improving financial capability in your community – and focus on addressing the needs and/or problems you identified in your assessment/evaluation. For example, if your goal is to reduce the number of unbanked individuals in your community, set a realistic target for how many people you would like to impact. Many communities have successfully leveraged BankOn and similar programs to achieve their targets. These programs are partnerships typically between banks/credit unions, community partners and government entities to provide access to low-cost, safe accounts and financial education for unbanked, usually low-income individuals.

   · The website joinbankon.org provides state, tribal and local data on the un- and under-banked and many resources on starting a Bank On initiative, as well as the ability to participate in discussions with other Bank On leaders.

3. Establish an awareness campaign and/or website to keep the local conversation growing and to provide tools to parents, families, and self-employed and micro business owners. For examples, see these websites:

   - indyscampaign.org

   - standbymede.org

4. Utilize business education and economic programs for self employed and local minority small businesses to help them manage their finances and grow their wealth. Programming could include:

   - U.S. Small Business Administration and SBA Direct: sba.gov

   - Startup America: www.s.co

   - Association for Enterprise Opportunity: microenterpriseworks.org

   - Kauffman Foundation: Kauffman.org

5. Support an area-wide (state, tribe, city) Earned Income Tax Credit (EITC) campaign to help low-income workers learn how to access their benefits.

   - Corporate Voices for Working Families offers free employer guides and EITC educational and marketing toolkits at www.corporatevoices.org.

   - Some examples from cities that have implemented EITC programs:

     i. Los Angeles: greaterlaeitc.org

     ii. Washington, D.C.: dceitc.org

6. Support initiatives to provide financial education at teachable moments. For example, some cities are incorporating FAFSA help with tax assistance provided at IRS offices for national VITA (Voluntary Income Tax Assistance) coalitions.

   - Ladder Up is an organization that demonstrates how this can work in practice: goladderup.org.

Financial capability in the workplace

1. Hold meetings and/or summits with state, tribal and local employers and encourage the adoption of employee benefits that align with the PACFC private industry recommendations.

2. Draft a formal recommendation that your state, tribal or local government adopt employee benefits/workplace financial capability programs for its own employees that align with the PACFC's "Proposed Recommendation Regarding Financial Capability Resources for Federal Employees," available here: http://www.treasury.gov/resource-center/financial-education/Documents/FINAL%20Federal%20Employee%20Recommendation%201-19-12.pdf

3. Encourage local employers to compete in the Workplace Leaders in Financial Education Awards, sponsored by the American Institute of Certified Public Accountants (AICPA) and the Society for Human Resources Management (SHRM). Learn more at wlife.org.

4. Encourage self-employed, micro- and small-business owners to utilize CDFI and credit unions to minimize banking fees, build their savings, and separate their personal and business transactions.

Other initiatives

The following ideas and initiatives may support more than one of the core areas of focus listed above (youth, access for the underserved, and workplace):

1. Create Financial Education Networks, whereby local nonprofits, educators, practitioners, librarians, government leaders and others get to know each others' areas of expertise and programming, and find opportunities to share best practices and maximize local resources. San Francisco and New York City provide Financial Education Network information and resources:

   · San Francisco: frbsf.org/community/issues/fensf.html

   · New York City: nyc.gov/html/ofe/html/providers/join.shtml

2. Be inclusive and further encourage partnerships by hosting financial literacy town hall meetings, roundtables, conferences, and listening sessions to share ideas, collaborate, and explore new ways to enhance local financial capability.

   See an example of a press release announcing a listening session in Indianapolis at www.bankonindy.org first-lady-of-indianapolis-to-host-listening-session-with-u-s-treasury-official-and-members-of-presidents-advisory-council-on-financial-capability/

3. Create a local "financial literacy corps" that provides a centralized local resource for information on financial literacy volunteer opportunities across the state/tribe/city.

4. Build interest in your work by leveraging existing public awareness campaigns, such as:

   · National Financial Literacy Month: whitehouse.gov/the-press-office/2011/03/31/presidential-proclamation-national-financial-literacy-month

   · Money Smart Week: chicagofed.org/webpages/education/msw/index.cfm

   · America Saves Week: americasaves.org

Step 6:
Measure your impact and adjust your programs accordingly

As with any successful initiative, it's critical to establish at the outset clear objectives, as well as clear milestones, benchmarks and metrics for measuring success. (See Step 4.) Consider whether the chosen goals are implementable and achievable, given economic realities and conflicting pressures for time and money.

If initiatives fall short of achieving the established goals, carefully evaluate which factors or elements of the program to adjust. Reconsider whether the goals themselves are realistic for your community. And regardless of whether you're meeting all your goals, be sure to share your findings and results with other jurisdictions so they can learn from your experience.

- National Endowment for Financial Education's research-based customizable Evaluation Toolkit offers methods to measure program impact. The toolkit is available here: http://toolkit.nefe.org

Resource Guide

Resource Guide

This list of resources is not intended to be exhaustive.

Organization	Resource Details	Contact/Info
Cities for Financial Empowerment Coalition	Cities for Financial Empowerment (CFE) brings together pioneering municipal governments from across the country that have begun to use their power and positions to advance innovative financial empowerment initiatives.	cfecoalition.org
Corporation for Enterprise Development	CFED programs test and refine promising ideas to find out what works. Programs include matching funds, IDAs, asset-building for children, self-employment tax initiative.	cfed.org
	In addition, the CFED Scorecard reviews state-by-state performance and policy measures across five areas: Financial Assets & Income; Business & Jobs; Housing & Home-ownership; Healthcare and Education.	cfed.org/scorecard
Council for Economic Education	CEE offers comprehensive K-12 economic and personal finance education programs, including the basics of entrepreneurship, consisting of teaching resources across the curriculum, professional development for teachers, and nationally-normed assessment instruments.	councilforeconed.org
Delaware's Stand by Me program	The Delaware Financial Empowerment Partnership (DFEP) is a joint venture of the State of Delaware and the United Way of Delaware, providing a package of financial empowerment services called $tand By Me.	standbymede.org

Resource Guide

Organization	Resource Details	Contact/Info
Financial Education Network of San Francisco	The Financial Education Network – San Francisco (FEN-SF) is a collaborative group of San Francisco's nonprofit service providers, philanthropic funders, and local public sector representatives dedicated to improving financial education services in the City.	frbsf.org/community/issues/fensf.html
Financial Literacy Center/ New York Stock Exchange Foundation	NYSE Foundation and the Financial Literacy Center provide free resources for employers and employees.	nyse.nyx.com/financial-fitness-kit
Financial Literacy and Education Commission	Free, unbiased resources from more than 20 federal agencies on array of financial topics.	mymoney.gov
First Nations Development Institute	Provides financial education training to Native communities and tribal governments.	www.firstnations.org
Gallup Hope Index	Measures financial literacy in relationship to hope, wellbeing, and engagement among U.S. students in grades 5 through 12.	www.operationhope.org/page/pgid/39
Indianapolis Campaign for Financial Fitness	ICFF is a coalition of public and private organizations that helps Indianapolis residents and their families manage their finances. The goal is to achieve the improved quality of life that accompanies financial stability at any income level.	indyscampaign.org
Join Bank On	Research your community's under- and un-banked stats, and learn how to start a Bank On program in your area.	JoinBankOn.org

Resource Guide

Organization	Resource Details	Contact/Info
Jump$tart Coalition for Personal Finance	Jump$tart is a national coalition of organizations dedicated to improving the financial literacy of pre-kindergarten through college-age youth by providing advocacy, research, standards and educational resources.	jumpstart.org
Money Milestones	Money Milestones are the 20 essential financial lessons that kids need to know as they grow. They're written in easy-to-understand language, aimed at parents and children, and organized into 4 key concepts per age group.	moneyasyougrow.org
National Congress of American Indians	Works with tribal leaders on training and technical assistance on significant issue areas including financial education. Also conducts a Tribal Exchange on the Stock Market.	ncai.org
National Endowment for Financial Education – consumer and educator resources	NEFE offers consumer resources, an interactive video sharing site, a high-school financial planning program, and a site dedicated to community financial education instructors.	smartaboutmoney.org spendster.org hsfpp.nefe.org www.financialworkshopkits.org
National Endowment for Financial Education – Resources for employers	NEFE provides employers with a research-based step-by-step process to increase retirement savings plan participation, particularly among low-income and female employees.	retirementtlc.org
National Financial Capability Challenge	Information about the National Financial Capability Challenge, a financial capability test for high-school students sponsored by the U.S. Department of Treasury.	challenge.treas.gov

Resource Guide

Organization	Resource Details	Contact/Info
National Financial Capability Study	The FINRA Investor Education Foundation commissioned this national study of the financial capability of American adults. The overarching research objectives were to benchmark key indicators of financial capability and evaluate how these indicators vary with underlying demographic, behavioral, attitudinal and financial literacy characteristics.	finrafoundation.org/capability usfinancialcapability.org
National League of Cities	NLC Bank On Toolkit for Municipalities Banking on Opportunity: A Scan of the Evolving Field of Bank On Initiatives.	nlc.org/find-city-solutions/iyef/family-economic-success/asset-building/bank-on-cities-toolkit www.treasury.gov/resource-center/financial-education/Documents/Banking%20On%20Opportunity%20Nov%2011.pdf
Native CDFI Network	Coalition of more than 69 members to help strengthen the Native Community Development Financial Institution industry through which a significant amount of financial education for Native communities takes place.	facebook.com/Native-CDFI-Network
SHRM and AICPA's Workplace Leaders in Financial Education Awards	Awards program that recognizes organizations with exemplary workplace financial literacy efforts to enhance employee financial well-being and encourages employers to implement and further develop financial literacy programs.	Wlife.org

Resource Guide

Organization	Resource Details	Contact/Info
United Way	In 2008, United Way initiated an ambitious 10-year plan to cut in half the number of lower-income families who are financially unstable. This site provides information about how local United Way organizations are helping drive financial stability in their communities.	unitedway.org/our-work/income
Wisconsin Governor's Council on Financial Literacy	Link to Council webpage, with mission and initiatives. Link to the Executive Order establishing the Council.	wdfi.org/ymm/govcouncilfinlit wdfi.org/_resources/indexed/site/ymm/govcouncilfinlit/ExecOrder24.pdf

Appendix

Appendix

**Steps for Launching a Local Financial Literacy/
Financial Capability Council**

1. **Identify a leader for the Council**
   Identify a leader or official within the jurisdiction who has the mandate, influence, and stature in the government and community to lead the Council effort. (For example, in San Francisco the effort is led by the City Treasurer; in New York City, the effort is led by the Commissioner of the Department of Consumer Affairs.)

2. **Recruit Council members**
   Identify influential government officials and/or elected officials, representatives of businesses (both financial and non-financial), non-profit organizations, academic institutions, private foundations and other individuals who are willing and eager to engage on the topic financial literacy, capability, and empowerment.

3. **Take official steps to create the Council**
   This could mean encouraging legislation to create the Council or encourage state, county or city executive branch leaders to create it by executive order. See examples of executive orders in the Resource Guide.

4. **Formally kick off the Council**
   Host a preliminary hearing and/or meeting in your area around the "State of Financial Literacy and Financial Capability." Announce the establishment of the Council and its charter.

5. **Focus the work**
   Choose two or three key areas of focus for the Council's initial energy. Form subcommittees in each of these areas. For example, the President's Advisory Council on Financial Capability is focusing on three key areas: 1) Youth financial education and capability; 2) Financial access for the underserved; 3) Financial capability through the workplace.

6. **Articulate clear goals and metrics**

   Create a core list of financial literacy and financial capability goals and objectives that will enhance the lives of community members.

   Examples: Every public school student in [jurisdiction] will complete financial capability education; 50% of all employers in [jurisdiction] will voluntarily implement financial education that aligns with U.S. Treasury Department's Core Competencies; [Jurisdiction] will move 60% of all unbanked individuals into the financial mainstream with bank accounts and/or direct deposit within 5 years; [Jurisdiction] will reduce the foreclosure rate by 40% within the next 18 months.

7. **Conduct and release an official research survey, study, or report on financial literacy and financial capability in your area**

   Leverage existing resources from states and other governments to determine which data is most critical in your jurisdiction. If resources are not available to conduct a unique study, leverage the state-by-state results from the FINRA Foundation's National Financial Capability Study. usfinancialcapability.org

8. **Stay connected**

   Invite federal agencies, federal officials and statewide officials to partner with state, tribal or local campaigns. Establish relationships with consortiums such as Cities for Financial Empowerment, so that your Council can share and learn from others.

9. **Be inclusive**

   Conduct "listening sessions" with local stakeholders such as youth, service providers, community organizations, employers, practitioners and others to better understand the issues and financial challenges faced by people in your community and to help drive and hone the Council's focus and energy.

The President's Advisory Council on Financial Capability would like to thank the following organizations for contributing their expertise, guidance and support in the creation of this document:

AARP Foundation

Accion Texas

Charles Schwab Foundation

Cities for Financial
Empowerment Coalition

Corporation for Enterprise Development

Council for Economic Education

Defense Credit Union Council

Delaware's Office of Financial
Empowerment

Economic Empowerment Initiative

Financial Education Network of
San Francisco

FINRA Investor Education Foundation

Financial Literacy Center

Financial Literacy and Education
Commission

Indianapolis Campaign for
Financial Fitness

Jump$tart Coalition for Personal Finance

National Congress of American Indians

National Endowment for Financial
Education

National League of Cities

Network for Teaching Entrepreneurship

New York Stock Exchange Foundation

Operation Hope

Society for Human Resources
Management

United Way

U.S. Conference of Black Mayors

U.S. Department of Education

U.S. Department of the Treasury

Wisconsin's Office of Financial Literacy

The following cities and counties:

Chicago

County of Hawaii

Los Angeles

Miami

Newark

New York City

Providence

San Francisco

San Antonio

Savannah

Seattle